THE NAP MINISTRY'S
REST DECK

50 PRACTICES TO RESIST GRIND CULTURE

Tricia Hersey

Welcome to your DreamSpace, a space free from the oppression of grind culture where you can heal, invent, imagine, and find liberation.

The *Rest Deck* is a tool for your rest practice. The intention of these cards is for you to see them as quiet portals for your deprogramming from grind culture. Grind culture is a collaboration between capitalism and white supremacy. It views human bodies as a tool for production and pushes an unsustainable machine-level pace that disregards the inherent divinity in us all.

May the energy of these cards support your resistance to grind culture. May they act as a guide to help you go deeper into the portal of rest. May they be a metaphorical blanket to swaddle yourself in warmth. This deck is for the soft places we want to hold close. The places that capitalism, white supremacy, patriarchy, and ableism have attempted to steal from us.

This deck makes space and is an opportunity to tap back into the pauses necessary to reimagine what it feels like to be free from exhaustion. Wrap yourself in ease. Rest.

We are experiencing a slow paradigm shift. Our collective rest is leading the change. It has always been time for justice. It has always been time to rest. At this very moment, someone is deciding to rest instead of pushing their souls into exhaustion. Let the cards in this deck be a witness to intention and become a daily connection to rest and resistance.

Rest is a form of resistance because it disrupts and pushes back against capitalism and white supremacy. We cling to this truth like a lifeboat in a raging sea. We cling to the power of collective care. We focus on our collective rest, opening the DreamSpace to allow us to invent and imagine a new world rooted in liberation. We are hopeful. We are grateful for rest.

HOW TO USE THIS DECK

This deck includes 50 rest cards. Each card has a rest affirmation on the front and a simple rest practice on the back.

These cards are ready for the resistance and available as collaborators. They are here to assist you in your liberation work. I invite you to incorporate these cards into your life in every possible way. Keep the deck next to your bed to refer to before you go to sleep, when you wake up, or before a nap, or in your bag to inspire a daydreaming moment. You can tuck the cards under your pillow, place them underneath the bed, or place a card next to you on the couch while you are napping. Hold them in your hands while daydreaming or resting your eyes. Pull a card and place it at your desk. Let each card become a focal piece in every room. Display them wherever you are. Conceal them like treasures. Find them hidden away in your books, in your dresser, or on your shelf or altar.

Here are a few simple ways you can use the cards to deepen your rest practice:

One Card Spread
ANSWERS + DECLARATIONS

This is a soft answer or a loud declaration. Shuffle the deck and spread the cards out in front of you. Close your eyes, let your hands move over the cards, and pull one when you feel it's time, when a direct action is needed for you to focus on during your day. Hold this one card close. Meditate and engage with the rest practice.

Two Card Spread
INQUIRY + CURIOSITY

This is an inquiry and a curiosity practice. Let this spread give inspiration for ways to reimagine what rest can be for you. Shuffle the deck and pick two cards, lay them out, and wait for a question to come to you. What do you need to know right now? How can you bring rest in closer to you?

Three Card Spread
IMAGINATION MOOD BOARD

To create your Imagination Mood Board, pull three cards and place them beside one another. Let this spread tell a story about the rest life you are imagining. Each card represents deep imagination work with the possibility to crack open the boundaries placed on us by a system that degrades our divinity via grind culture. Imagine with them. Rest with them. Tap into the power of each card for as long as you need. As we deprogram from the brainwashing of grind culture, repetition and practice are necessary. Repeat daily. Rest with the spread whenever you need inspiration.

Let this deck be a companion on your rest pilgrimage. A pilgrimage is a journey to some sacred place. Rest is a sacred place. The body is a sacred place. Time is a sacred place. During a pilgrimage, things are worked out in the physical and spiritual worlds. You go on a pilgrimage to reclaim your time and body. You go on a pilgrimage to be changed. Let the existence of this deck taking up space in your home and heart be evidence of embodied change.

May a space to daydream and slow down open to you. May you realize the power of snatching rest because this culture will not give it to you. Our rest is a resistance message, a slow, meticulous love practice filled with grace, mercy, rage, power, and care. We must continue deprogramming from grind culture. We must continue not turning away from our own terror. We must deconstruct around the ways we uphold grind culture. We must wake up.

—Tricia Hersey

Tricia Hersey is an artist, a poet, a theologian, and a community organizer. She is the founder of The Nap Ministry, an organization that examines rest as a form of resistance by curating sacred spaces for the community to rest via Collective Napping Experiences, immersive workshops, performance art installations, and social media. Tricia is a global pioneer and originator of the movement to understand the liberatory power of rest. She is the creator of the Rest Is Resistance and Rest as Reparations frameworks. Her research interests include Black liberation theology, womanism, somatics, and cultural trauma. Tricia is a Chicago native and currently lives in South Georgia.

Text copyright © 2023 by Tricia Hersey.

All rights reserved. No part of this book may be reproduced in any form without written permission from the publisher.

ISBN 978-1-7972-1576-1

Manufactured in China.

MIX
Paper | Supporting responsible forestry
FSC™ C017606

Art by Paula Champagne.
Design by Lizzie Vaughan.
Typeset in Brandon Grotesque, Noe, and Warnock.

10 9 8 7

Chronicle books and gifts are available at special quantity discounts to corporations, professional associations, literacy programs, and other organizations. For details and discount information, please contact our premiums department at corporatesales@chroniclebooks.com or at 1-800-759-0190.

Chronicle Books LLC
680 Second Street
San Francisco, California 94107
www.chroniclebooks.com

CHRONICLE BOOKS
SAN FRANCISCO